SCOOBY-DOO!
and the
Truth Behind
WEREWOLVES

BY MARK WEAKLAND
ILLUSTRATED BY DARIO BRIZUELA

CAPSTONE PRESS
a capstone imprint

Published in 2015 by Capstone Press,
A Capstone Imprint
1710 Roe Crest Drive
North Mankato, Minnesota 56003
www.capstonepub.com

CAPS33044

Library of Congress Cataloging-in-Publication Data
Weakland, Mark, author.
Scooby-Doo! and the truth behind werewolves /
by Mark Weakland ; illustrated by Dario Brizuela.
pages cm.——(Unmasking monsters with Scooby-Doo!)
Summary: "The popular Scooby-Doo! and the Mystery Inc. gang
teach kids all about werewolves"——Provided by publisher.
Audience: Ages 6-8.
Audience: K to grade 3.
Includes bibliographical references and index.
ISBN 978-1-4914-1795-9 (library binding : alk. paper)
1. Werewolves—Juvenile literature. 2. Monsters—Juvenile
literature. 3. Curiosities and wonders—Juvenile literature. I.
Brizuela, Dario, illustrator. II. Title. III. Title: Werewolves.
GR830.W4W43 2015   001.944——dc23
2014029118

Editorial Credits:
Editor: Shelly Lyons
Designer: Ted Williams
Art Director: Nathan Gassman
Production Specialist: Tori Abraham

Design Elements:
Shutterstock: ailin1, AllAnd, hugolacasse, Studiojumpee

The illustrations in this book were created traditionally, with
digital coloring.

Thanks to our adviser for her expertise, research,
and advice:
Elizabeth Tucker Gould, Professor of English
Binghamton University

Printed in the United States of America in
Stevens Point, Wisconsin
092014   008479WZS15

Scooby-Doo and the gang were returning from a
walk in the park. Suddenly, Scooby-Doo perked up his ears.
"What's wrong, Scoob?" asked Shaggy.
"Rerewolf!" barked Scooby. "Up there!"
"Really?" asked Velma.
"Are you sure?" asked Fred. "Do you know what a werewolf is?"

"Maybe," said Daphne. "Stories say they live in houses and apartment buildings—just like humans. Werewolves are found all around the world."

"How do people become werewolves?" asked Shaggy.

"Legends tell us some people become werewolves through magic," said Velma.

"Others change when a werewolf bites them," added Fred. "Or when they drink water that a wolf has touched."

"When do werewolves change from human
to wolf?" asked Shaggy.

"Only at night," said Fred.

"When the moon is full," said Daphne.
"Like tonight. Look for a werewolf in the
moonlight, and listen for its howling."

"Like, do werewolves have superpowers?" asked Shaggy.

"You bet," answered Daphne. "Legends say they are really strong."

"And don't forget about their senses," said Velma. "They have extraordinary vision, hearing, and sense of smell."

"Werewolves are vicious hunters," said Daphne.

"True," said Fred. "And once they taste blood, they crave it."

"Also, unless they die while in human form," said Velma, "werewolves are immortal."

"They rever die?" gasped Scooby. "Ruh, roh!"

"Rolfsrane?" asked Scooby.

"A plant with a beautiful purple flower," said Velma. "It's very poisonous. That's why people don't grow it in flowerbeds."

Time for a review. What looks human but can change into a flesh-hungry wolf under a full moon?" asked Fred.

YOW!

"Rerewolf!" shouted Scooby.

Fred looked at Shaggy and laughed.

"Boy is this burrito hot!" cried Shaggy.

GLOSSARY

burrito—a Mexican food that is a tortilla rolled around a filling

curse—an evil spell meant to harm someone

immortal—able to live forever

legend—a story handed down from earlier times; it is often based in fact, but is not entirely true

transform—to change form

vicious—fierce or dangerous

READ MORE

Jeffrey, Gary. *Werewolves.* Graphic Mythical Creatures. New York: Gareth Stevens Pub., 2011.

Troupe, Thomas Kingsley. *The Legend of the Werewolf.* Legend Has It. Mankato, Minn.: Picture Window Books, 2011.

INTERNET SITES

FactHound offers a safe, fun way to find Internet sites related to this book. All of the sites on FactHound have been researched by our staff.

Here's all you do:

Visit *www.facthound.com*

Type in this code: 9781491417959

 Super-cool stuff! Check out projects, games and lots more at **www.capstonekids.com**

INDEX